Dogs Dressed Up
and No Place to Go

Written by

Emily Thornton   Erika Cornstuble
Ali Pohn   Paul Seaburn

new seasons®

I'm afraid if I don't see some improvement in the quality of dog food around here, I'm going to have to let you go.

We ARE smiling.

We thought these costumes would help clarify who's in charge around here.

Brutus was into extreme sports—
well, as much as you can be
when you only weigh three pounds,
can't swim,
don't own a skateboard,
get hives in the cold....

The invitation said
red tie and tails.

You pups have it so easy.
In my day, we had to take
ourselves for walks...
in the snow...uphill...
both ways.

I don't know, Santa,
you're just *furrier* than I expected.

Are you sure
this is how the Big Bad Wolf
got started?

Hey! You over there—
you wanna piece of me?

The invitation did say costumes…
didn't it?

A hummingbird just attacked me.

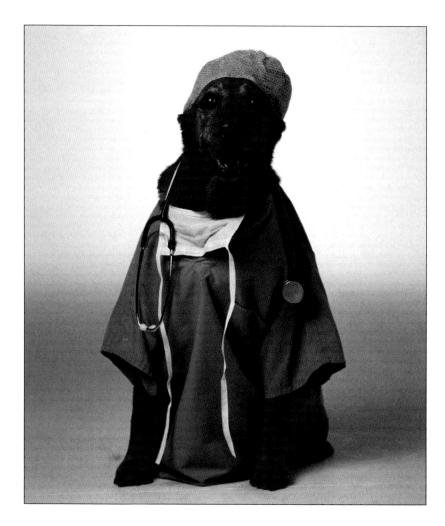

Good news:
The bone has been successfully
removed from the backyard.

Daily averages:
- 4 walks
- 2 runs
- 5 stolen bones

Sadie waits for her signal
to go on in "The Muttcracker."

Oh, yeah,
those two cute poodles
are definitely checking us out!

I've been dreaming about this day
ever since I was a puppy
playing with white toilet paper.

I'll wear the hat and bow tie,
but don't even try to get
those tap shoes on me.

Of all the people
who could have adopted me,
I get a guy
who still remembers vaudeville.

I've skipped
"doggy paddling"
and gone directly to
"doggy boating."

Stop me if you've heard this one before:
A collie, a poodle, and a Shih Tzu
walk into a bar....

How youuuu doin'?

Arrgh...
I guess I dug up one too many
buried treasures.

I didn't catch the spirit of the season.
It attacked me.

I may be color-blind,
but I still view life
through rose-colored glasses.

Skip "Happy Birthday."
Just bring on the cake!

I'm more the
"laughing on the inside"
type.

A dog without a hat
is like a fish without a bicycle.

Pilot to copilot:
Fasten your seat belt;
it's going to be a bumpy ride.

Stick around—
I'm getting ready to do
the Mexican Hat Dance.

Good grooming is no substitute
for good breeding.

Trick or treat!

It was a tough decision:
Spend the money on Botox™
or on LASIK surgery?

The other white mutt.

This isn't what I meant
when I wished for nicer buns.

Virtual cat chasing:
All of the flavor,
none of the guilt.